THE INDIVIDUALIST

Understanding the Enneagram 4

Asa Eccleston Kibilski

CONTENTS

THE LONGING FOR AUTHENTICITY: UNVEILING THE ENNEAGRAM FOUR

The world is a vast tapestry of personalities, each a unique blend of thoughts, emotions, and instinctive urges. Within this vibrant mix, there exists a type marked by a deep yearning for authenticity – the Enneagram Type Four, also known as 'The Individualist.'

At the very core of the Individualist beats a heart consumed by the desire to be seen, understood, and appreciated for their true essence. There's a profound dissatisfaction with the ordinary, a restless search for something more meaningful, more unique. They are the poets, the artists, the romantics of the world, their gaze often fixed on the profound and the bittersweet within the human experience. A sense of melancholy frequently hangs over a Type Four, a bittersweet longing for the elusive beauty they perceive just beyond their grasp.

This inner landscape, marked by a rich emotional life, is also one of contrasts. Individualists are deeply sensitive, capable of experiencing both the heights of joy and the depths of despair with extraordinary intensity. They possess a gift for empathy, easily tuning into the unspoken emotions of others, and they are drawn to the complexities of the human heart. However, this sensitivity also renders them vulnerable, sometimes causing them to feel as though they experience the world without the protective layer of skin that others seem to possess.

Fours often feel a sense of being fundamentally different. There's a belief that no one could truly understand the intricate workings of their inner world, leading to a sense of isolation. To combat this perceived separateness, they cultivate a unique identity – a carefully crafted expression of their individuality that sets them apart from the crowd. Whether through art, fashion, or lifestyle, they seek to etch their unique mark upon the world. However, there's a fine line between healthy self-expression and the creation of a persona that obscures rather than reveals their true selves.

Fours have an innate understanding of the power of beauty and aesthetics. They find solace and inspiration in music, art, literature; anything that stirs their soul and ignites their imagination. The beauty they perceive in the external world becomes a mirror for the beauty they crave to find within themselves. But, they are also drawn to the melancholy, the bittersweet, often resonating deeply with themes of loss, unrequited longing, and profound sadness.

The deep longing for authenticity is the driving force of The Individualist. They seek to know themselves deeply, to uncover the layers of their being. There's a fervent desire to live a life untainted by pretense or superficiality, a life that reflects the truth burning within their hearts. This journey is rarely easy and can be fraught with challenges, but for the Type Four, it is a journey worth taking. It's on this path that they discover their true gifts, embrace their authentic selves, and begin to build a life of meaning and purpose.

THE HEART OF MELANCHOLY: EXPLORING THE EMOTIONAL CENTER

If the Type Four were a landscape, it would be a land of swirling tempests and vibrant sunsets, a place where the very air seems to thrum with a symphony of emotions. Fours belong to what's known as the 'Heart Center' of the Enneagram, dominated by feelings of shame, longing, and a pervasive sense of something essential missing from their lives. This emotional intensity is both their greatest strength and a source of their deepest challenges.

At the very root of a Four's emotional landscape lies a profound sensitivity. They experience the world on an amplified frequency – joy bursts forth in dazzling color, while pain cuts deeper than a blade. Their emotional capacity is a double-edged sword. On one hand, it grants them an extraordinary ability to empathize, to feel acutely and deeply with others. They can sense the hidden sorrows and unspoken joys in a way that's often baffling to other personality types. It is precisely this sensitivity that makes them gifted artists, musicians, and healers – their talent lies in their capacity to translate the complexities of the human heart into forms that resonate with others.

However, this heightened sensitivity also leaves the Individualist vulnerable to emotional overwhelm. What might be a minor irritation for another can feel like an unbearable wound to a Four. Their inner world is often in a state of tumult, with emotions shifting and changing with bewildering speed. They have a tendency to ruminate on negative experiences, replaying them over and over in their minds, dissecting them with a relentless intensity. This can lead to spirals of negativity and a pervasive sense of melancholic dissatisfaction that colors their whole experience of life.

The emotional hallmark of the Four is a yearning for a connection that feels eternally out of reach. This sense of longing often stems from feeling fundamentally misunderstood and different from those around them. Even within a loving family or surrounded by friends, the Four can experience a lingering sense of isolation, a belief that their inner world is so complex that no one could truly comprehend it. This sense of lack gives rise to the feeling of having a hole in their soul that nothing in the external world seems able to fill.

The Enneagram teaches us that often our core weaknesses are rooted in distorted versions of our core strengths. Fours, with their capacity for depth and emotional connection, are prone to falling into the trap of emotional dependence. They can fixate on finding that one person who 'gets them', believing this will finally bring them the peace and fulfillment they crave. This dependency, often masked by an outward appearance of fierce independence, can lead to unhealthy patterns in relationships and ultimately intensify their underlying fear of being inherently unlovable.

THE CRAVING FOR MEANING: THE HEAD CENTER AND THE QUEST FOR IDENTITY

While emotions roar like an ocean within the Type Four, a parallel storm rages in their minds. Fours are also part of the 'Head Center' of the Enneagram. Like their Head Center siblings, Types Five and Six, they have a deep need to make sense of the world and their place within it. Their quest for meaning is entwined with a near-obsessive focus on identity and a desperate need to feel unique and significant.

The Individualist's mind is rarely still. Their thoughts race tirelessly, analyzing their experiences, dissecting their emotions, and sifting through a relentless stream of internal dialogue. Fours are driven by an insatiable curiosity about themselves, a thirst to understand the depths of their being and find a cohesive narrative that encapsulates who they truly are. They are fascinated by the complexities of their own psychology and the intricacies of human behavior in general. Hours can vanish in introspective pondering, where they attempt to unravel the tangled threads of their past to illuminate their present.

This preoccupation with identity is rooted in a deep insecurity. Many Fours struggle with a fear that if stripped of their unique persona, there would be nothing remarkable at their core. They strive to cultivate a sense of self that is distinct, original, even a little eccentric or unconventional. They may be drawn to artistic self-expression, using it as a way to externalize their rich inner world and project an image that marks them as different. This focus on uniqueness and meaning is their shield against the fear of dissolving into the faceless masses, of being simply ordinary.

Fours have a powerful imagination, often finding sanctuary in rich internal worlds. This imagination fuels their creativity and allows them to see beauty in places others might overlook. However, it can also become a dangerous refuge. When reality feels harsh or disappointing, an Individualist may retreat into the comforting embrace of fantasy, escaping into daydreams where everything aligns with their desires. While a rich imagination is a gift, when used as an avoidance strategy, it becomes a barrier to building a fulfilling life in the real world.

The Four's struggle for a sense of meaning and their fascination with their emotional depths can manifest as a tendency towards introspection that borders on brooding. They risk getting lost in their own thoughts, caught in a cycle of self-analysis that paralyzes them rather than illuminating a path forward. Their minds, powerful tools for creativity and understanding, can become traps, leaving them ensnared in a web of overthinking and negative self-talk.

THE YEARNING TO CONNECT: THE BODY CENTER AND THE PARADOX OF INTIMACY

While Type Fours are primarily associated with a tempestuous inner landscape of emotions and thoughts, the Enneagram reminds us that all types have a relationship with all three centers of intelligence: Heart, Head, and Body. While the Body Center is often their least dominant, it plays a pivotal role in the Individualist's journey towards integration and wholeness.

The Body Center is associated with instincts, groundedness, and our sense of presence in the here and now. Fours, often lost in the world of thoughts and feeling, can struggle to feel truly embodied, to experience a sense of ease and security within themselves. Their connection to their physical selves can be tenuous, and their instincts may feel unreliable or even confusing to them. This internal disconnect can contribute to their sense of alienation from the world and from themselves.

Beneath the Individualist's longing for deep emotional connection often lies a paradoxical fear of intimacy. This fear is rooted in a deep vulnerability, a sense that to be truly seen and known for all their flaws and complexities would be unbearable. Fours can be intensely self-conscious, plagued by the belief that they are fundamentally defective in some way. To protect this wounded inner core, they may unconsciously build invisible walls around themselves, keeping others at a safe distance even as they yearn to be truly understood.

This internal battle between the desire for connection and the fear of exposure can manifest in a pattern of push-and-pull in their relationships. They may crave closeness yet feel overwhelmed by it, longing for deep intimacy yet somehow sabotaging relationships just as things start to feel secure. This internal conflict can be immensely frustrating to the Four and deeply confusing to their loved ones.

The Body Center is also where we hold our sense of anger, a powerful but often suppressed emotion for Fours. Individualists, with their focus on emotional authenticity, might assume they have no issues with anger. However, they often struggle with expressing anger in a healthy and assertive way. The fear of damaging their connections may lead them to swallow their anger, letting resentment build up silently beneath the surface. Alternatively, their anger may explode in bursts of intense emotion that feel uncharacteristic and leave both themselves and those around them confused and hurt.

Fours, like all beings, have a fundamental need for physical safety and security. Feeling grounded in their bodies is essential for developing a sense of inner stability and navigating the turbulent waters of their emotional landscape. Developing healthy practices like mindful movement, exercise, or body-centered therapies can create a gateway for Fours to reconnect with their physical selves and begin to release pent-up energies in a healthy way. Building a sense of embodied presence allows them to step out of their whirlwind of thoughts and into the present moment, fostering a sense of peace within the storm.

TWO SIDES OF THE COIN: THE WINGS OF THE INDIVIDUALIST

The Enneagram is not merely about a single, rigid type, but rather an entire spectrum of interconnected possibilities. While all Fours share certain core traits, their unique personalities take on different shades depending on the influences of their neighboring types - Type Three and Type Five. These neighboring types, known as 'wings', add subtle complexity and nuance to the core Individualist experience.

The 4w3 Wing: The Aristocrat's Envy

Fours with a strong Three wing possess a noticeable drive for achievement and recognition that sets them apart from their more introspective Four siblings. While all Fours crave significance, the 4w3 is drawn to external validation as a way of confirming their specialness. They possess a flair for the dramatic and an ambitious streak, desiring not just uniqueness but also a degree of success or admiration from others. They are often more image-conscious, putting effort into cultivating a persona that aligns with their idealized sense of self.

The Three influence can bring a much-needed boost of energy and action to the Four's internal world. They may have an entrepreneurial spirit, transforming their creative passions into tangible projects or expressions in the world. Their ambition can help them to overcome the Four's natural tendency towards inertia and self-doubt. The 4w3's gift lies in their ability to bridge the gap between their rich inner landscape and the external world, sharing their unique vision in a way that resonates with a wider audience.

However, the influence of the Three can also amplify the Four's sensitivity to comparison and fuel envy. The Three's focus on success can trigger the Four's deep-seated fear of being ordinary or unremarkable. Seeing the apparent ease with which others achieve their goals or garner attention can lead to a painful spiral of self-critique. The path for the 4w3 involves learning to channel their ambition into healthy expressions and to differentiate their own definition of success from external markers of achievement.

The 4w5 Wing: The Bohemian's Melancholy

Type Fours with a strong Five wing are the introverts of the introverts. They are less drawn to external accomplishments and far more invested in their inner landscape of thoughts and emotions. The world can feel overstimulating, and they find solace and a sense of safety in retreating into the sanctuary of their own minds. 4w5s are often drawn to intellectual pursuits, finding pleasure in exploring complex ideas, analyzing literature, or immersing themselves in their chosen creative fields.

The Five wing brings a degree of detachment and objectivity to the Four's emotional experience. This allows them to observe their inner world with a sense of curiosity, analyzing their emotions rather than being wholly consumed by them. They have a deep thirst for knowledge and a gift for synthesizing information into unique insights. The 4w5 has the potential to be an incredibly original thinker, their rich emotional world serving as fuel for profound creative expression.

The influence of the Five can create a tendency towards isolation and withdrawal. While 4w5s have a deep capacity for connection, their social energy is limited. They may struggle to maintain friendships or feel easily overstimulated by socializing. They have to be mindful not to completely surrender to the allure of their inner world, risking detachment from the realm of human connection and the nourishment it provides.

THE ARISTOCRAT'S ENVY: UNDERSTANDING THE 4W3 WING

For the Type Four with a strong Three wing, life often feels like a grand stage, with the world watching their every move. The 4w3 is the extroverted face of the Individualist; charismatic, ambitious, and image-conscious, they exude a captivating blend of vulnerability and strength. The melancholic longing of the Four intersects with the Three's drive for success, creating a complex and often contradictory internal landscape.

The 4w3 brings a flair for the dramatic, a certain artistic intensity to their presentation. They are less likely to fade into the background than their more introverted Four siblings. Driven by a desire to express their unique vision, they may pursue creative careers that place them in the spotlight, becoming musicians, actors, designers, or entrepreneurs. There's a desire to be not just different, but to leave a legacy, a mark on the world that reflects their individuality.

The Three wing adds a competitive edge to the Four's sensitivity. The 4w3 can be deeply affected by comparing themselves to others, leading to strong pangs of envy when they witness the successes or validation received by their peers. While all Fours can fall into the trap of comparison, the 4w3 feels its sting with particular intensity, often accompanied by harsh self-critique and a relentless drive to improve. The challenge for the 4w3 lies in differentiating between their true creative aspirations and the culturally conditioned markers of external success that don't always align with true fulfillment.

The Three's focus on image can be both a blessing and a

curse for the 4w3. On the one hand, it grants them a sense of style and presence, allowing them to express their creativity with confidence. However, there's also a risk of becoming overly focused on external appearances, using image as a way to mask deeper insecurities or create distance from others. Striving for achievement can become a way to numb the underlying fear of not being inherently worthy of love or admiration.

Yet, the Three wing isn't only a source of striving and envy for the Four. It brings a much-needed dose of action and assertiveness. The 4w3 is less likely to become paralyzed by self-doubt, with their ambition pushing them to take risks and put themselves out there. They find a powerful outlet to channel their emotional intensity into tangible projects and creative endeavors. The 4w3 possesses the rare ability to translate the ethereal beauty and complex emotional truths of their inner world into expressions that have a powerful impact on others.

THE BOHEMIAN'S MELANCHOLY: UNDERSTANDING THE 4W5 WING

The Type Four with a strong Five wing is the true bohemian, the quiet philosopher-poet of the Enneagram. Their existence is steeped in a blend of brooding melancholy and a deep thirst for knowledge. They are the observers, the ones who watch the world from a slight emotional and intellectual distance, analyzing human experience with both curiosity and a hint of sadness.

For the 4w5, privacy is paramount. The world often feels too harsh, too overwhelming for their finely-tuned senses. They find refuge in solitude, feeling safest when immersed in their inner world of thoughts, emotions, and creative pursuits. Their homes may become sanctuary-like spaces reflecting their unique tastes and sensibilities. They often possess a vast reservoir of knowledge on niche interests, which they may become quite passionate about.

While Fours with a Three wing may yearn for the spotlight, the 4w5 prefers the shadows. They are less concerned with external validation and far more interested in uncovering the hidden depths within themselves. Their creativity tends to be deeply personal – private journals of poetry and prose, paintings that may never be shared with the world, or music born from late-night bouts of melancholic inspiration.

The Five wing amplifies the Four's tendency towards introspection and analysis. 4w5s spend copious amounts of time dissecting their emotional experiences and pondering philosophical questions. They possess a gift for observing the nuances of human behavior and extracting deeper meaning from their encounters with the world. Their ability to hold both a cool intellectual detachment and a deep well of feeling gives their creative work a unique flavor, infused with wisdom and poignant honesty.

However, the 4w5's tendency to retreat into their minds can ultimately become a source of isolation. They risk becoming overly detached, forgetting that meaningful connection is an essential need. Fear of emotional vulnerability can lead to them keeping even loved ones at a safe distance. The 4w5 must learn to trust the strength of their inner emotional landscape enough to occasionally let others in, allowing themselves to be seen and supported.

The Five influence also brings about a certain inertia in the Four. While the 4w5 has a rich imagination and deep creative capacity, they may struggle to move from ideas to actions. Fear of being judged, of having their creation fall short of their internal ideal, can paralyze them, causing a buildup of creative energy with no outlet. Building practices that allow them to feel grounded in their bodies, supported by others, and courageous enough to express their unique vision into the world is key to their integration.

THE SHADOW'S EMBRACE: THE UNHEALTHY EXPRESSIONS OF A FOUR

The Enneagram teaches us that our greatest strengths often contain the seeds of our greatest weaknesses. The Individualist, with their rich emotional depths and longing for authenticity, is no exception. When stress builds, Fours can spiral downward into unhealthy expressions of their type, losing sight of their core gifts and becoming trapped in destructive patterns. Recognizing these 'shadow' aspects is an essential step on the path towards integration and wholeness.

One unhealthy manifestation of the Four is a tendency to indulge in envy and self-pity. Their focus on what they perceive to be lacking in their lives becomes all-consuming. They compare themselves to others, seeing only what appears to be effortless success, joy, or love bestowed upon those around them. This fuels an intense sense of injustice, a feeling that the universe is cruel for denying them the happiness they see reflected in others. This envy transforms into a bitter stew of self-deprecation, where the Four becomes their own harshest critic.

As stress mounts, Fours can adopt an almost romantic attachment to suffering. Rather than taking steps to address their unhappiness, they cling to it, wearing their melancholy like a badge of honor. There's a distorted belief that their pain is what makes them unique, that it gives them a kind of tragic beauty. They may actively reject things that bring them joy, convinced it will dilute their artistic sensibility or make them less authentic. The Four in this state becomes an almost caricature of the tortured artist, losing touch with their innate capacity for joy and vitality.

Under stress, Individualists can also become emotionally volatile. Their suppressed feelings build up over time, creating an unstable internal pressure that eventually explodes in bursts of anger or tearful accusations. They may lash out at loved ones, blaming others for their dissatisfaction and pushing away those offering support. This emotional volatility stems from a deep fear of being unmasked, of others glimpsing their perceived unworthiness beneath the carefully constructed image of the Individualist.

The unhealthy Four can become incredibly self-absorbed. Their inner landscapes become so tumultuous that they lose sight of the needs of others entirely. They may become demanding, expecting partners, friends, or family to cater to their emotional needs constantly. Attempts to establish healthy boundaries are met with accusations or dramatic displays of pain. The Four, in this state, loses the empathy that is normally one of their greatest strengths and comes to believe that their suffering is so profound that others could never truly understand it.

While exploring the shadow aspects of the type can be sobering, it's important to remember that these are not permanent states of being. With self-awareness and intentional work, it is possible for Fours to move away from these unhealthy expressions and cultivate their many gifts. Recognizing the signs of downward spirals is the first step towards choosing a healthier response.

THE CREATIVE SPARK: UNLEASHING THE GIFTS OF THE INDIVIDUALIST

At their healthiest and most integrated, Type Fours are a gift to the world. They are artists, poets, healers, and truth-seekers whose unique perspective enriches our understanding of the human experience. Their ability to touch the hidden depths of emotion and translate them into forms of beauty is a powerful reminder that even within our suffering, there is a wellspring of creativity and resilience.

Perhaps the Individualist's most profound gift is their capacity for empathy. When they move beyond their own emotional storms, Fours have an extraordinary ability to connect with the joys and sorrows of others. They see what's hidden beneath the surface, sensing the unspoken longings and unhealed wounds within the hearts they encounter. Their presence has a soothing quality, as they mirror back the authenticity of another person's emotions in a way that feels implicitly validating and understood. It's in this space of deep connection that true healing can occur.

Fours have an innate appreciation for the beauty in the world, even amidst darkness and pain. They find solace in the melancholy chords of music, the poignant turn of phrase in poetry, the fleeting beauty of a sunset. Art, in all its forms, speaks to their souls in a way that words sometimes cannot. Their receptivity to beauty isn't simply an aesthetic preference; it's a profound spiritual need, a way of connecting to the ephemeral threads of meaning woven into the fabric of life.

Healthy Fours are deeply introspective, possessing a rich understanding of their own complex emotions and motivations.

This self-awareness allows them to extend compassion towards others, understanding that behavior is often driven by unseen pain and fear. Rather than judging harshly, they see beneath the surface with empathy, recognizing the common threads of longing that unite us all.

At their best, Individualists possess a profound capacity for creative expression. It's through their art, however it manifests, that they find catharsis for their deepest emotions. Their ability to translate the nuances of the heart into poetry, music, dance, or visual art is what makes their creative work touch the souls of others so deeply. For Fours, creativity is not merely an outlet - it's a sacred act, a way of externalizing the storm within and transforming their pain into something transcendent and beautiful.

When Fours learn to balance their rich emotional depths with a grounded sense of self, they become unstoppable forces of authenticity. Their vulnerability becomes a source of strength, allowing them to connect with others at a profound level and inspire those around them to step into their own truth. They are a reminder that our deepest longings and our hidden sorrows are not something to be hidden away, but are the wellspring from which creativity, connection, and healing emerge.

FINDING HARMONY:
GROWTH AND INTEGRATION
FOR THE FOUR

The Enneagram isn't intended to be a prison, locking us into rigid patterns. True understanding of the types offers us a pathway toward greater wholeness and freedom. For the Type Four, integration involves harnessing their remarkable strengths, managing their shadow aspects, and drawing on the wisdom of other types within the Enneagram, especially their lines of connection to Type One and Type Two.

Harnessing the Gifts of Type One

Fours connect to Type One, the principled perfectionist, through a path known as the 'line of growth'. Type Ones have the ability to bring a sense of groundedness and discipline to the Four's sometimes chaotic inner landscape. Embracing the One's focus on integrity teaches the Four the importance of aligning their actions with their deepest values. Their desire for authenticity guides them to live with increasing honesty, no longer needing to create complex personas that hide their true selves. The One's influence helps the Four move away from self-indulgent melancholia and into actionable steps that foster a greater sense of personal responsibility.

Learning from Type Two

Type Fours also have a line of connection to Type Two, the helper archetype. Twos offer the Four the gift of warmth and a focus on the needs of others. This connection balances the Four's tendency towards self-absorption. Healthy Twos model how to establish healthy boundaries from a place of love and self-respect, a much-needed lesson for Fours who fear rejection and abandonment. Witnessing the Two's generosity of spirit softens the Four's sometimes hardened heart, reminding them of the joy and fulfillment that comes from offering support and connection to others without the need for constant reciprocation.

The Growth Path for Fours

- **Honoring the Body:** Learning practices that help them feel embodied and grounded is essential. Mindful movement, body-based therapy, or regular exercise can help Fours release pent-up emotional energy and tap into the instinctual wisdom of their bodies.
- **Self-Compassion:** Fours are often their own harshest critics. Cultivating a practice of self-compassion is vital. This means being patient with their intense emotions, remembering that vulnerability is not weakness, and treating themselves with the same kindness they would extend to a dear friend.
- **Finding Joy:** Fours must learn that authentic joy and soulful depth can coexist. Consciously making time for activities that bring them pleasure allows them to see that happiness doesn't diminish their depth, but rather replenishes their creative wellspring.
- **Healthy Comparisons:** Recognizing their tendency towards harmful comparisons, they can begin to turn that energy into inspiration instead. Witnessing the achievements of others can spark a sense of self-confidence and motivation, fueling their ambition instead of their self-critique.
- **Building a Support System:** The Four's path of integration involves learning to trust others and allow themselves to be truly seen. Building a network of supportive loved ones who know not just their strengths but their shadow aspects too, creates a sense of safety that allows for deeper healing and vulnerability.

The journey towards integration is an ongoing one. Fours must learn to accept themselves wholly – with their deep emotional capacity, their yearning for beauty, their occasional flare of drama, and yes, even their moments of melancholy. It is in embracing the totality of their being that they discover the wholeness they so desperately crave. Through self-awareness, compassion, and intentional action, the Individualist can harness their profound gifts, build deep and lasting connections, and cultivate a life brimming with authenticity, creativity, and a deep sense of purpose.

THE POWER OF VULNERABILITY: BUILDING HEALTHY RELATIONSHIPS AS A FOUR

For the Type Four, the longing for true connection lies very close to the wound of feeling fundamentally different. Their sensitivity and depth make them incredible repositories of empathy, but it also leaves them vulnerable to deep feelings of isolation and a nagging fear of rejection. While building authentic relationships can be challenging, it is a fundamental need and one of the primary pathways towards personal growth for the Individualist.

One of the greatest obstacles to healthy relationships for a Four is the unconscious belief that something is inherently unlovable about them. This core wound of their type leads to a pattern of self-sabotage. They may push others away with intense displays of emotion, subconsciously testing their loyalty, waiting for the inevitable moment when they are abandoned. Or, they may withdraw, fearing rejection so deeply that they keep others at a safe distance before any real connection can take place.

True vulnerability is the antidote. Fours must come to understand that their depth, even the parts they've been conditioned to believe are too intense or too messy, is actually the very thing that draws people to them and fosters deep connection. This doesn't mean baring their hearts and souls with reckless abandon. Rather, vulnerability in the context of a healthy relationship means gradually allowing another person to see their true nature, with its flaws, sensitivities, and its radiant beauty.

The path to healthy relationships for a Four involves several key steps:

- **Understanding Attachment Styles** Fours often fall into anxious or avoidant attachment patterns, making it difficult to find healthy emotional security in relationships. Recognizing their attachment patterns helps them address the root causes of their relationship challenges and develop healthier coping mechanisms.

- **Practicing Open Communication:** Fours can fall into a pattern of 'feeling into' what others are thinking and becoming hurt or reactive based on their assumptions, leading to unnecessary conflict. Learning to communicate their needs, fears, and emotions directly with clarity and compassion is crucial for healthy relationships.

- **Managing Expectations:** The Four's tendency towards idealization can set them up for disappointment. Developing realistic expectations, accepting that all relationships will involve some conflict and challenges, fosters resilience and deeper bonds. Instead of longing for the perfect love that absolves them of their pain, a healthy Four learns to find beauty and connection within an imperfect, but authentic, relationship

- **Setting Boundaries:** Fours can become emotionally drained when they constantly feel responsible for the well-being of others. Learning to set healthy boundaries is crucial for safeguarding their energy. This involves confidently saying 'no' to taking on the burdens of others while remaining open to offering support in a balanced and sustainable way.

- **Accepting Love:** Fours must learn to truly believe that they deserve love and connection, even if they feel their emotions are messy or their journey of authenticity doesn't look the way they thought it would. Healing the core wound of unworthiness allows them to receive the love and support they deeply crave without fear or self-sabotage.

Finding a partner who celebrates their depth, offers groundedness to their emotional storms, and who is willing to walk the path of growth alongside them is invaluable to a Four. It is through the healing power of love and connection, nurtured with patience and vulnerability, that the Individualist finds a safe haven for their tender heart and builds the fulfilling life their soul craves.

BEYOND THE COMPARISON TRAP: EMBRACING YOUR UNIQUENESS

Fours are haunted by the specter of comparison. They crave uniqueness but are constantly measuring themselves against others, fueling a cycle of envy and inadequacy. In a world that bombards us with idealized images of success and happiness, it can be difficult for any personality type to find contentment within themselves. For the sensitive and self-critical Four, this battle is even more pronounced.

The root of the Four's comparison trap lies in their deep-seated fear of being ordinary. In their quest for meaning and significance, they may fixate on what they perceive to be lacking in their own lives, leading to envy of those who seem to possess the qualities or achievements they long for. This comparison becomes a form of self-torture, breeding resentment and eroding the Four's self-esteem.

Fours often make the mistake of conflating external markers of success with true authenticity and fulfillment. They may admire the confidence of a social butterfly, the effortless style of someone seemingly always in the spotlight, or the professional achievements of someone highly recognized in their field. The Four mistakenly believes that mirroring these external qualities will finally lead them to the inner peace and sense of significance they so desperately seek.

The way out of the comparison trap is a paradoxical one – Fours must embrace their own fundamental ordinariness. This doesn't mean surrendering to mediocrity or giving up on their creative aspirations. Rather, it requires them to find beauty, meaning, and a sense of self-worth within their flawed, imperfect, and yet beautifully unique human existence.

Here are a few potent practices to break free from envy's clutches:

- **The Gratitude Shift:** Fours naturally focus on the lack instead of appreciating what's present. A daily gratitude practice helps them retrain their focus towards abundance. This may mean appreciating the simplest things - a beautiful sunset, a nourishing meal, or a heartfelt conversation.
- **Redefining Success:** Challenge the societal definition of success. For an Individualist, true success lies in the alignment of their values, creative expression, and how they choose to express their authentic self in the world.
- **Celebrating Your Gifts:** Fours often take their talents for granted. Regularly identifying their unique strengths - their empathy, creativity, or ability to see beauty where others don't - builds a solid foundation of self-appreciation.
- **Practicing 'Inspirational Comparisons':** Instead of harmful comparisons that lead to self-critique, consciously choose to be inspired by others. Seek out those who embody their authentic expression courageously – it can spark motivation and fuel healthy ambition.

The Four's path towards liberation from envy involves recognizing that their true specialness is woven into the fabric of their everyday existence. It lies in the way they perceive the world, the unique emotions that color their experience, and in the creative expression that flows through them. It is by embracing the ordinary that the Individualist discovers their truly extraordinary nature.

THE ART OF AUTHENTICITY: EXPRESSING YOUR TRUE SELF

The Type Four's life is, in essence, a relentless quest for authenticity. Their every breath seems an outcry against the mundane, the cookie-cutter, the soulless. They reject inauthenticity with an intensity that can be both inspiring and unsettling to those less driven by the longing for truth. However, translating this inner yearning into authentic self-expression in the world can be a complicated path.

One of the challenges Fours face is their tendency to construct elaborate personas to mask their perceived flaws. Fearful of being discovered as fundamentally unworthy, they may create an image based on what they believe will win validation and admiration from others. It's a performance aimed at hiding the parts of themselves they deem too broken or too messy to ever be acceptable. However, true authenticity can never be found in a facade, no matter how carefully constructed.

The path towards authentic self-expression begins with the courageous act of turning inwards. It involves taking a long, clear-eyed look at all the parts they've been desperately trying to hide. This journey into the heart of their shadows requires them to develop a deep well of self-compassion. In the safe container of self-kindness, they can begin to dismantle old beliefs about their unworthiness, the stories they've told themselves about being too much or not enough. Only when they learn to fully embrace themselves can they begin to show that true self to the world.

Creativity is the Four's native language. It's through their art, however it manifests, that they give shape and form to the intangible landscape of their inner world. The creative process is an act of excavation. They pull their truths from the depths, weaving their longing, pain, and fragments of beauty into poetry, music, dance, or visual art. Sharing their creations with others is a powerful act of vulnerability, a defiant stand against the pressure to conform, a celebration of the unique and the irreplaceable.

Authenticity for the Four also involves living in alignment with their core values. This means saying 'no' to things that feel disingenuous, even if it means occasionally being misunderstood. It means walking away from roles, situations, or relationships that dim their inner light, even if it means facing disapproval or the fear of rejection. When rooted in their values, the Four's decisions become affirmations of their inherent self-worth.

Living a life of true authenticity is an ongoing practice, not a fixed state of achievement. Fours must constantly navigate the tension between their inner world and societal expectations. There will be times of messy vulnerability as they shed old ways of being and learn to own even the parts of themselves that are rough around the edges.

Authentic self-expression is both a form of rebellion and a homecoming. It's a defiant rejection of the world's insistence on conformity and a brave acceptance of the complex, tender, and radiant being within. It's when the Four's true brilliance emerges, shining a light that can illuminate the path for others who long to step into the wholeness of their true selves.

BEAUTY IN BROKENNESS:
FINDING MEANING IN SUFFERING

The Type Four has a unique relationship with suffering. They resonate with the bittersweet notes of melancholy, finding a strange beauty in life's imperfections. But what if they could find not just an artistic connection with suffering, but profound meaning and growth? This chapter explores how the Individualist can transform their pain into a source of strength, compassion, and resilience.

Fours often wear their suffering like a badge of honor. There can be a subconscious belief that it's their pain that makes them special. While it's true that a Four's capacity for depth is born from their experience of both joy and sorrow, clinging to suffering ultimately becomes a prison, inhibiting growth and isolating them from the full spectrum of human experience.

The first step in transforming suffering is to differentiate between pain and suffering. Pain is an unavoidable part of being human. It could be emotional pain from an experience of loss, rejection, or disappointment, or it could be physical suffering. Suffering, on the other hand, is optional. It's the story we create around our pain, the narrative we repeat in our minds on a loop that amplifies our anguish and prevents healing.

For Fours, whose minds are powerful story-making machines, this distinction is crucial. Recognizing their tendency to dwell on their pain, they can begin to turn their gift for introspection into an act of compassionate witnessing. It means observing their painful thoughts and emotions with non-judgmental awareness, allowing them to surface without getting caught in the undertow of negativity. This mindful observation creates a spaciousness around the experience, preventing their identity from becoming fused with their wounds.

One of the most powerful antidotes to suffering is the search for meaning. Instead of wallowing in self-pity, Fours can question their pain, asking "What can this teach me? How can I grow from this experience?" Suffering can reveal hidden strengths, expose outdated beliefs, and deepen their understanding of themselves and others. By finding value, however small, in even the most challenging life experiences, Fours shift their relationship to pain, turning it into a catalyst for personal transformation.

The Four's extraordinary empathy is a gift to the world, but it's only sustainable when they learn to fill their own wells of compassion. Their natural inclination is to focus on the suffering of others, but to truly be present for loved ones facing their own struggles, they must first offer compassion to themselves. Cultivating practices of self-care, mindfulness, or spiritual connection becomes essential for refueling their own well of kindness and resilience.

Suffering can crack open hearts in a way that prosperity sometimes cannot. As painful as it may be, facing hardship builds a profound empathy for the shared human struggle. Fours, with their finely-tuned awareness of pain and their innate understanding of the bittersweet beauty of life, are uniquely positioned to transform their own experiences into a beacon of hope for others struggling through the darkness. It's through their courage to be vulnerable, their willingness to share their journey of healing, that they become sources of inspiration and support for those who need it most.

THE JOURNEY OF WHOLENESS: A LIFE OF PURPOSE AND PASSION

Type Fours, in their heart of hearts, long for a life of significance, one that truly aligns with their deepest passions and reflects the richness of their inner world. This final chapter offers a roadmap to crafting that life, integrating the lessons of self-awareness, vulnerability, creativity, and resilience into a path of wholeness. Wholeness for the Individualist is not just an idea, but an ongoing journey, one filled with purpose, authenticity, and deep joy.

The Path to Purpose

The Four's path to purpose starts with self-exploration. Identifying core values, passions, and talents that feel intrinsically true is a guiding compass as they map out their life's course. While Fours naturally gravitate towards creative pursuits, purpose isn't tied exclusively to artistic self-expression. It may unfold through teaching, healing, activism, or even seemingly ordinary jobs performed with extraordinary heart. Purpose for a Four is about channeling their unique energy and perspective into something that feels meaningful and aligned with who they are at the core.

Balancing Ambition and Acceptance

Fours must dance between healthy ambition and a deep acceptance of where they are now. Their desire for significance can be a powerful motivator, but it must be balanced with recognition that growth and fulfillment are not destinations but processes. Comparing themselves to where others are on their path is a sure-fire recipe for dissatisfaction. Instead, celebrating even small wins and recognizing their own unique trajectory builds inner strength and confidence for the long haul.

Honoring the Inner Critic

Self-doubt is a constant companion for the Four. However, instead of being paralyzed by their inner critic, they can choose to engage with it curiously. Recognizing that critical voice as a product of old fears and wounds opens up space for a kinder, more supportive internal dialogue. Instead of accepting self-criticism as truth, Fours can question these inner voices and counter negative self-talk with affirmations of their inherent worthiness and potential.

Cultivating Joy

Fours often feel a pang of guilt when experiencing joy, as if it somehow diminishes their depth or the aesthetic appeal of their melancholy. Joy is the fuel that nourishes creativity. Intentionally cultivating experiences that light them up is not a frivolous act, but one of self-care and a potent way to counter the negativity bias that can sometimes overshadow their world. Finding joy in the simple – laughter, sunshine, the beauty of nature – rejuvenates their creative spirit and deepens their capacity to experience the full spectrum of life's textures.

Nurturing Connections

Healthy relationships are the lifeblood of wholeness and fulfillment. Fours can honor their need for solitude while nurturing meaningful bonds with loved ones who accept them fully, flaws and all. Building a network of supportive individuals who offer both groundedness and encouragement allows Fours to blossom in their authenticity, knowing they are cherished even when their emotions are tempestuous.

The Gift of Service

The Four's unique perspective and empathy are gifts to the world. Finding ways to contribute meaningfully, whether through volunteerism, acts of kindness, or through their creative expression, fuels a profound sense of purpose. Witnessing how their gifts positively impact others heals their own wounds of unworthiness and builds deep, lasting fulfillment.

Life is rarely as smooth as the Four's idealized vision. There will be setbacks, moments of self-doubt, and old patterns re-emerging. But it is by embracing their whole journey, with its highs, lows, and everything in between, that the Individualist truly finds the sense of wholeness they so deeply crave. Wholeness is a lifelong pursuit, a dynamic state of being that encompasses acceptance, growth, joy, purpose, and a defiant commitment to living with the fullest, most authentic expression of their beautiful and complex hearts.